Common Ground

A James R. Hepworth Book

Common Ground

Poems by John Daniel

CONFLUENCE PRESS, INC. /1988

Acknowledgements

Some of these poems have appeared in the following publications: *The Amicus Journal, Calapooya Collage 11, Clearwater Journal, The Country Poet, CutBank, High Country News, KSOR Guide, Northern Lights, Not Man Apart, Oregon East, Poetry Now, Sawmill, Sequoia, Snapdragon, The South Dakota Review, The Southern Review, Southwest Review, Wild Oregon, Wind/Literary Journal,* and *Writers' Forum.*

"Of Earth" first appeared in *The North American Review.*

Earlier forms of "Note to a Young Fisherman" and "December in the Oregon Desert" appeared in a chapbook, *Third Season/Seven Poets.* Special thanks to Sandra Gullikson, publisher of Clearwater Press, Little Rock, Arkansas.

An earlier form of "The Burden" was anthologized in *The Beast in a Cage of Words.* Thanks to Alan Cohen, Sun's Nest Press, Belchertown, Massachusetts.

"The Longing" was anthologized in *The Pushcart Prize VIII: Best of The Small Presses.*

I wrote many of these poems between 1982 and 1987, while I was a Wallace Stegner Fellow and Jones Lecturer at Stanford University. I am grateful to the Creative Writing Program, to all my friends and teachers at Stanford, and especially to Ken Fields, Denise Levertov, Simone Di Piero, and John L'Heureux.

ISBN 0-917652-56-8 Cloth / 0-917652-73-8 Paper
LIBRARY OF CONGRESS CARD NUMBER 87-73557

Publication of this book is made possible by grants from the Idaho Commission on the Arts, a State agency, and the National Endowment for the Arts in Washington, D.C., a Federal agency.

Cover Art and Illustrations by Edward Livingston
Production and Design by Tanya Gonzales

Published by

Confluence Press, Inc.
Lewis Clark State College
8th Avenue & 6th Street
Lewiston, Idaho 83501

Distributed to the trade by

Kampmann & Company
9 East 40th Street
New York, New York 10016

This book is for my mother, Elizabeth Hawes Daniel, and in memory of my father, Franz E. Daniel.

CONTENTS

ONE

TWO

THREE

FOUR

ONE

One Place To Begin

You need a reason, any reason—skiing, a job
   in movies, the Golden Gate Bridge.
Take your reason and drive west, past the Rockies.
When you're bored with bare hills, dry flats
   and distance, stop anywhere.
Forget where you thought you were going.

Rattle through the beer cans in the ditch.
If there's a fence, try your luck—they don't
   stop cows.
Follow the first hawk you see, and when the sagebrush
   trips you, take a good look before you get up.
Catch a sockful of prickly-pear spines—the desert
   gets by without government.

Crush juniper berries, breathe the smell, smear
   your face.
When you wonder why you're here, yell as loud
   as you can and don't look behind.
Walk. Your feet are learning.

Admit you're afraid of the dark.
Soak the warmth from scabrock, cheek to lichen.
The wind isn't talking to you. Listen anyway.
Let the cries of coyotes light a fire
   in your heart.
Remember the terrible song of stars—you knew it
   once, before you were born.

Tell a story about why the sun comes back.
Sit still until the itches give up, lizards
   ignore you, a mule deer holds you in her eyes.
Explain yourself over and over, forget it all

when a scrub jay shrieks.
Imagine sun, sky, and wind the same, over your
    scattered white bones.

                        You're close now.
Wander up a dusty ravine until your nose
    smells something different.
Climb to the green grass, the stand of aspens.
Squirm your toes in black mud, with the tracks
    of hooves and paws.
Drink. The face that rises to meet you
    has been waiting for you to come home.

For The Fire

In cold morning sun
I raise my maul, aim
for the calm pooled rings
of a round of pine.

Two halves spring from the block,
fresh-faced grain
on glaring snow. Drunk
with the dangerous musk of pitch

I swing with all the hard love
I know, slick with sweat,
grunting with the drive
of the eight-pound steel.

The split pieces settle
heavy in my arms
as I walk to the shed, dry lips
on bare pine flesh. Rough

and gentle as any father,
I stack them to sleep
for that ice-still morning
I will come to them, lonely,

asking for their warmth and song.

The Great Horned Owl

He holds his hurt like a fresh kill,
dares me to take it. With a child's triumph
I grip the talons that know only gripping,
his hooked beak slashing at my leather gloves,
ragged bone jutting from the limp left wing.

In his shed he listens to the barnyard hens
he used to terrify. When I open the door
he blinks in the flashlight glare and seizes me
in his great yellow eyes. Alone with the dark
he stirs my gift of cold mice. He does not eat.

He was the shadow against the stars,
the blur at the edge of my headlights,
the ghost who discarded headless sparrows
in the dust outside my gate, the voice
that called in the pines when nothing else spoke.

Four days of death are all he can bear.
I find him raking his claws in the heavy dirt
that will not let him go. In the morning
specks of straw are stuck to his eyes.
He hangs in my hand like nothing, a husk,

as if all he was had been life itself.
Long after dark, with only coyotes awake,
I hear his voice. Beneath Orion, barefoot
in the dry grass, I raise my arms in the cold
south wind, close my eyes and almost fly.

Note To A Young Fisherman

for Andy Hamilton

Before your rod arched
with that unseen strike
and the taut line sang
through the surface of possibility,
the ocean within you was still,
brilliant with what could be,
ready to be surprised.
You might have reeled
a mermaid from that water.

It's not the lure, it's that
glint of mind that gets the fish.
Cast yourself far from shore,
don't fear drifting in darkness.
Visions will flash from the depths.
Understanding will tug, slip away,
tug again. And someday
the one you've been waiting for
will swirl to your surface,
fighting hard as it must,
the wise and beautiful one
you somehow knew was there.

Why I Listen To Family Stories

When Aunt Frances sits up tall in her chair
and her eyes loom dark and huge in her lenses
and she announces it's time I got married,
"Remember your Uncle Tell," I say, and Frances
laughs like a girl—

          because Tell Daniel made
the best harness in Missouri, but never learned
to drive his own Model T, so Frances,
six feet of schoolgirl, steered it to his shop
on the square one steamy August evening
to bring Tell home for dinner, and Tell,
a gentle man who smelled of cool leather,
said Frances should turn right instead of left—
or left instead of right, she isn't sure now,
but she's goddamned sure how she turned on Tell
with all six feet full of scorn—

          "You don't
need a brain to be a Daniel, only a good
pair of ears, 'cause there's always another
Daniel around to tell you what to do."

Reading

I've been glancing over as I turn each page
for nearly an hour now, and the lizard's
still crouched outside the window, its blunt head
tilted toward the dark. What's it waiting for?
No insects in this cold, only a few leaves
blowing by, only the October night
and this five-inch dragon, gripping the sill
and growing stranger the longer I stare.

The rabbit's nerves I understand—we had
the same mother once, a furry something
who stayed alive through luck and jumpiness
in the fern-swamps of Tyrannosaurus.
When coyotes howl my scalp prickles, a call
of my own turns over in its sleep. Even
the birds, reptilian themselves, are bright
and soft in their masquerades of feathers,
they warm their young—

                              but this lizard's belly
must be as cool as window glass. Its blood
moves glacially. It's part of the night
some silent way I've forgotten. It's home,
it waits for nothing. I put down my book,
ease closer across the carpet: I see
the palpitation in its waxy throat,
the splayed fingers, tensed elbows, the tail
curved on a leaf—and the blunt head flicks,

one yellow side-staring eye takes hold of me.
I do know it somehow, it's a sunken dream

I can't quite raise. *Lizard*, I say, as if
the sound could clarify, as if to stir
some answer from the stillness of its gaze,
not curious, not fearful, but aware.
We stare through glass, taking in what we can,
each a vague trouble in the other's eye.

A Calf

for Karen Hamilton

1

Quiet with the pain of her choked womb
the heifer stands stiff-legged.
The boys watch as their father
breaks her water, reaches in:
the milky-tongued head slides stubbornly out
but the shoulders catch. He chains
the forelegs and all of us pull,
feet braced on posts
straining flat with the ground
as the heifer humps her back and groans—
in a liquid rush the calf
comes free, slaps the cold April mud.

2

He shivers on his side, a big
black-and-white. The legs
that won't lift him to suck
stir feebly on straw. His mother
tongues and tongues his sopped fur dry.

3

On the bathroom floor he strives
at the bottle, dies down
into troubled rest. We hear
his nasal bleats all night,
the weightless skitter of hooves.
What's wrong with him? Geoff asks at breakfast
and we can't say—strangled too long
half-born, maybe, or flawed
from the seed. When we lift him,
the legs hang like ropes.

4

Three days he lolls in his heat-lamp womb,
as we bring bottles
and encouraging words.
Give up, we don't say.
If you could live
you would have walked.
You were steaks and soupbones anyway.
We study his black and white splotches
like a map we don't know how to read.

5

An earlier calf, even bigger,
we could only deliver in bloody pieces.
But that was a finish.
This gloom goes on, the young safely born
but broken inside his clean colors.
The forehead curls are fluffy and thick,
the pink hooves harden gray.

6

He seizes the nipple, he sucks
with such yearning violence
Nathan grips the bottle with both hands.
Then he's gone again,
slumped on his side, staring
after something too far to see.
In the quiet each morning
we come for his corpse
but he will not die, he will not live.
His mother lows at the pasture fence.

7

The boys are yelling, on their knees—
the calf's forelegs buckle
but he stays half up.
They lift him again
and skidding on the slick floortiles
he stands, takes one step
on shaky legs too long for him,
steps again, and flops on his face.

8

Steady in the grass he takes the tit,
stub-tail twitching, then
follows her across the windy field
toward the others where they lie and stand.
He stops, looks to one side
with lowered head, square rump high,
then bolts to catch up,
something old and sure in his legs,
something that knows the ground by heart.

First Light

I stand at the woodstack
with owls still calling,
four deer in the frozen pasture,
the tops of the tall pines
incandescent with sun.

This is the way it begins.
We come back to ourselves
always here, now, in the light
divided from dark by no clear line,
that returns us to our own keeping.

I could drop these hunks of pine,
melt into morning like a coyote,
see the house, from far,
as one more thing. In this light
anywhere would be home.

The owls answer each other.
The deer watch, listen.
We are wakeful together,
as if keeping an old promise
to meet here, in this first light.

The Elm In November

The slow labor of summer
is finished, the yellow weight
delivered to ground. Twigs
jittering, buoyant with wind,
the elm comes round once more
to the grace of emptiness.
It enters the cold unburdened,
its life withdrawn inside
the solitude of its dark limbs,
exact pattern against gray sky,
the spare shape of enough.

TWO

The Sound Of Mountain Water

Hiking the ridgecrest
you mistake it for wind—you know
it began long before,
a whisper that finally woke you.
Retrace the trail
till you're dead or crazy,
you won't find a line
between sound and silence.

Closer, you're sure for a moment
it called your name.
Your mind chases
slippery syllables, the fluent tongue
of snowmelt on granite
that forgets what it starts to say.
You remember camps
on other streams—you're weary,
hungry for dinner.

Awake by cold ashes
you've arrived at last—
moon, pines, that naked voice.
On the trail next morning
you're so filled with its song
you forget that the stream is miles
behind—then suddenly
you hear the dry silence.

Journey

The mountains were going somewhere
when they buried their faces to rest.
Wind remembers—urges, scolds,

but the mountains in their dream
feel only a sad pale woman
stroking them deeper in sleep.

Water shouts a while and gives up,
learns silence far from home,
wanders back, in white, to die.

Trees know in their roots
where the mountains were going,
but sunlight makes them forget.

Frogs remember at dusk, announcing it
all together, and hawks
have always known but don't care much.

People believe the mountains are dead
because they lie so still,
but the mountains are only sleeping.

Snowmelt wakes them grain by grain—
in the cold rush they remember
the journey, in the cold rush they go on.

Unidentified Critter In The Locust Tree

I heard a hummingbird
revving its motor
in the locust tree.

When I stuck my head
through the leaves
to see what kind it was,

it propped itself on air
two feet from my face,
took a good look

and flew like hell.

December In The Oregon Desert

Lucky thing Peter Skene Ogden
had a man along to count the days
and remember Christmas when it came to pass—

Scripture words, the warmth in mind
of eastern hearths. A man could backslide
tramping these flats where only

the scabrocks haven't found cover,
the heathen storms haranguing,
digging nails into your faith. This space

could wear out eyes and ears
and leave you wandering wild as sage,
your pale skin cured red,

reading signs in antelope bones,
following a prophet tumbleweed
over snow and snow to some barefisted peak

where you shiver in the spell
of a scatter of stars one bright as the next,
as coyotes howl in the continental dark—

and the quiet floods back, stars and snow,
and that faint word of wind born over and over
in which everything here has a place except you.

Joshua Trees

These bent trees that Mormons saw
as the prophet waving, waving the way
through desolation to a better land

I see as hunched arthritic geezers,
ballerinas, monks who've long forgotten
how not to pray, and I'd have to watch

until mice made a home in my skull
to stop seeing man—as if to be real
they have to be human, as if

these shaggy trunks, these spike-leaves
stirring in steady dry wind
showed any way except their own,

as if this rocky sand they rise from
half an inch a year, the only trees,
this soil that gives them all they need

to put forth clumps of heavy bloom,
each limbtip bursting in creamy flower,
as if this ground they're rooted in

were not itself the promised land.

Beginnings

No god broke these billions of stones,
or knows where they will be, or what,
in a billion years. No higher power
commanded cactus from the stones,

or magenta blooms from the cactus pads.
The darting hummingbird drinks *here*,
now *here*, its only map the flowers
themselves, and sparrows dip and veer

among the sharp-spined yucca trees
with precision they don't need to plan.
They find their way, as the swirling breeze
finds its own way, and the clouds

through their immensity of light,
and these are not the works of mind
but mind itself, mind waking to say
stone, cactus, flower, wind—

speaking these things, and finding its way.

Vaquero

Down the drywash mouth of Tajo Canyon,
three days hiking, the desert flushed
and fragrant with afternoon rain—
a corral of cactus logs, one horse,
a board and sheetmetal shanty
patched against a palo verde tree.

His name is Alberto Gomez, he spends
much time here herding four hundred cows.
Oildrum stove, a stack of mesquite;
his hat and three beef flaps
hang from the limb that holds up the roof.
He sees me look, heats a black skillet.

Down in the sand with cigarettes,
thick coffee, he leads me
in English as bad as my Spanish
through the next canyon south,
and the next and the next, as a woman
sings cracked and faint on the radio

and the sheetmetal roof sings rain.

At Dusk

In the stillness lying like a shadow
on my camp, the fir forest wakes.
Twig-cracks, rustlings, a grouse
drums three times.

Tracks in old snow
led up the white-water creek today,
deeper into wilderness
than I knew how to follow.
Cougar went there, and now crouches
somewhere on a granite crag
knowing all that moves
in this deepening dusk

where I am a blind man learning to hear.
The creatures stirring with small sounds
know their way
in the darkness of trees.
The grouse has journeyed through eons
to drum three times
and fall still—

I rest in silence,
one life passing in the presence
of trees, as the trees
pass in a green blur over granite,
and the mountains rise
and weather away
in tides only the sky can see,

blue world in a wilderness of stars.

A Crossing

...*my only swerving*—
—W.S.

Blinded in light the deer froze—
my fender crumpled, hurled her
down the bank.

                I found her thrashing,
the broken legs trying to run.
Pleading, hating her ruined life,
I grabbed a rock and hammered her head,
again, and again—

and stood breathing hard
in the silence of stars and pines,
smeared rock a perfect fit
in my fingers.

               Again my headlights
tunnelled the dark. I gripped
the wheel, one of the strangers
who kill at any crossing,
without the stomach to pay dead life

the respect of an honest hunger.

Oklahoma

In the twilit fields a single hawk glides,
oil pumps slowly bow and rise,
and an old barn sags
under too much sky.
Cottonwoods line the county roads,
stand in clumps by vacant houses,
their long backs bent in the wind.

This is the land no one needed, ignored
by trappers and the trundling wagons,

the land we filled with Cherokee and Creek,
Seminole, Choctaw, Chickasaw,
and the others we broke
from the earth like grasses—Modoc, Cheyenne—
as we found our West, and swarmed,

the land we came back to
when we ran out of ground, the land
we fenced, plowed, planted, and cursed
as the wind blew dark in the sky, the soil
drifting away and we after it,
hungry and looking.

              Now,
through this vastness of fields and distant lights
we drive the unwavering highway
twenty miles over the limit, passing
something we have not yet found, a stillness
at the level of land—
in the dry red dirt of Oklahoma,
something waiting for us to arrive.

Hanaupah Canyon

Piñons grip the canyon walls, shadows pooled
on hot red stone, roots
thrust deep in cracks
where the seed chanced in—
each twisted tree at home in its place,
the giant sharp-edged boulders
perfect where they've tumbled,
gardens of prickly-pear growing among them,
by the water that glistens down slick granite
to pool and sink into sand.

I wasn't sure what I wanted, jarred
in the rush of stinking traffic,
loud with little jealousies and fears,

but this old clear truth
that sends and sends itself,
that sings in the mountain's cool open heart
is plenty—billions of years
before anything learned how to see or hear,
the glistening slide, the sound
of drops in a pool.

That Earth, of all the ways of being
should happen just this way—
what I hold in mind
of the work ongoing here
is a drop of all that I can't know,
that fills me and flows through,
as clear and aching
as this water I hold streaming through my hands.

THREE

At Thirty-Five

Mustard crowds the barbed-wire fence,
the entire hillside thick with light
and glowing brighter as the pale sky
goes dim. The single oak is hazed
with April leaves. Across the valley
children call, quick strokes of sound.
A wavering cloud of sparrows passes,
a kestrel hovers on beating wings—
impossibly much, and impossibly,
not enough. I need more tonight
than the bare glory of what's given,
I need to rub this moment in mind
for the shimmer of meaning I almost see,
I need the boy who stood shivering once
in a different field, hands clenched
at his sides in the clammy dusk
as he silently burned into mind
the whippoorwills, silhouettes of trees,
the bright clear blue of the west—
I'll remember, he whispered, *even
when I'm dead I'll remember this*.

A Year Among The Owls

1

At dusk an owl sits blinking
in the oak
as students walk home, alone
and in pairs
through the silent quad,

lifts its tail, craps white
and flies
to the ridge of the red-tiled roof—
silhouette,
turning its head
one way then the other,

still there
as it grows too dark for me to see.

2

You can't see the owl at night,
but it sees you.

Sometimes at dusk you can see it,
but it saw you first.

In daylight you can haul yourself up
and peer in its hole. It's asleep.

You're still not important,
even though you've climbed a tree.

3

With the call of one owl the stillness
of lamplight and desk is changed
to the stillness of forest and night.
From the nest in the pine, the hollow oak,
from barns, mineshafts, seacliff ledges
they glide forth, soundless, seeing and hearing
with a clarity we could not bear, a field
of bright knowing across the dark land.

4

In the classroom we talk about our poems.
Outside in the rain
the owl in the oak and the owl in the palm
call to each other.

5

I assumed you were still
when you gave your call.
I didn't know until now,
watching you in the palm,
that your white throat puffs
like a tuba player's cheeks,
and you lean forward
very carefully it seems
placing your voice into air.

6

I am like the owl in two ways:
I sleep in the day,
I move into homes I did not build.

Some think the owl is lazy.
Some think the owl is smart.

7

Tired of reading while the owl calls,
I open the door and answer:

hoo hoooo   hoo hoo

It is silent the rest of the night.

8

When it comes I hope it's at night
in the fields, a sudden shadow
against stars. In the grasp
of that vision much clearer than mine,
I'll rise with my fading light
in the great silent motion of wings.

9

As I heard the owls in my sleep
I kept drifting to the surface
and downward again.
Toward morning I dreamed of a boy
blowing a song on an empty bottle,
over and over, alone
in the dark but not afraid,
trying to get it just right.

Recovery

The *whap* on the glass door that brought me
stumbling with hangover and Sunday paper
is a goldfinch, lying on the step
unconscious, throat pumping.

Weightless against my finger,
wind ruffling and smoothing the yellow feathers,
each filament distinct.
Clenched claws, the eyes half-shut.

I sit reading my paper, nearly asleep
until the goldfinch startles
us both, awake in one twitch
turning its head

then hopping—two inches, two inches,
down off the step—*wait*—across concrete
hopping, bright yellow, the black wings flick
into the orange tree.

Carefully I part the boughs, the cool
shaded fruit: ants, a caterpillar, bits
of blue sky. Then through the leaves
I see myself in the glass door,

my head in a tree. The rest of the morning
I sit in the sun eating oranges,
my headache easing, the wind
just lifting the hair of my arms.

After Hearing From A Friend

Since you called, I've been walking
the wet grass listening to frogs,
their steady chorus pulsing along
until a few at a time they hush,
and hush, and the last frog chirps
kind of silly for a while and quits.

My loud footsteps, wind in the trees,
stars scattered like farmlights
lonely on the prairie...

are you *there*?

                                are you *there*?

are you *there*?

                are you *there*?

                        are you *there*?

                                are you *there*?

—and every damn bubble-throated frog
in the meadow is chirping its heart out.

Who knows why they sing, but tonight
it sounds like celebration, tonight
I think the only reason they stop
is for the pleasure of starting again.

At A Party, Three Years Later

Gold hair still hangs below your waist,
combed with glances in any room.
It was a cool cave to hide in,
damp tangled grass, it feathered
my cheek when we walked in the wind.
My elbow caught it against the sheet—
you hurt, but I wouldn't trim it
when you handed me scissors.

South of Shasta we hit a rabbit.
My sleeves were wet with your tears
before you could drive again.
Sweet, sweet salt—the times I matched you
cry for cry, a pair of drunks
who wouldn't go home.
We rolled helpless in that warm bath,
hoping it was love.

The world, all elbows, tugs hard
at us both. But the weather
has left us now. Friendliness creaks
in the old connections. We ask
how we are, hands empty at our sides,
hanging straight and useless as your hair.
When talk dies we have only
our smiles, fixed like gashes.

Tonight In The Quiet
I Think Of My Father

1

When those two kids smashed my snowfort
because we were *nigger-lovers* who walked
with signs in front of the amusement park
you told me I should have fought back

when I quit the football team I said
it took too much time from study
but really I didn't like the hitting and horseplay
you turned without a word and hoed your tomatoes

when I dropped out of Reed
you didn't even have my grades to be proud of
I told you I wouldn't go into the army
and you said you believed in me

but I wondered
if you thought it was really just fear
I wasn't sure myself

2

in my letters I told you that LSD
would change the world   that Beatles songs
told all the truth we needed

and you in your room at Menninger's Clinic
trying to quiet your shaking hands

trying to forget   if you ever remembered
how Jim and I found you asleep on the stairs
how we steadied you from restaurants   how you insisted
on playing first base in our game
and dropped every throw grinning like a fool

and those nights you didn't know I listened
burning in bed crying *out get out*
as you and mom shouted downstairs
your heavy feet creaking the floor   I imagined
you seizing her shaking her

when I tiptoed down to turn off the hi-fi
you were slumped in your rocking chair

3

but you did it   you lived ten dry years
on AA black coffee and Chesterfields

that must have been harder than anything else
harder than leading the picket line
in those textile strikes in the thirties
when the bosses stood on the roof of the mill
aiming a machine gun down
then called in their brass-knuckled goons

harder than facing those Tennessee thugs
and their bullet that stopped
in the paper-crammed wallet
in your coat pocket over your heart

when you took me with you preaching the Union
to solemn men in high school gyms
I didn't get the words but I saw how they listened
how they crowded to shake your hand

I didn't know then
that loneliness met you wherever you travelled
the nighttime quiet of another hotel
Jim Beam burning your throat

those ten sober years
we wrote letters about gardens and politics
shook hands averting eyes   watched baseball together
carefully holding our silence
like something precious between us

4

by myself in a new town tonight
I'm thinking of you in New York in the twenties

on your own from Missouri   your father dead
I see you in lamplight reading your books
walking the crowded streets   your work
growing clearer and clearer inside you

I see you all the time these days
the way I sit with elbows resting on thighs
the way I turn up the volume for Beethoven's Third
the way I curse and brood when the wrong team wins

father
whatever you gave me or failed to give
somehow in confusion I'm finding my way

it's easy to write this
to a man who can't read it
but tonight I believe I have enough courage

tonight if you were sitting in this quiet with me
I think I could be a better man
than either of us was

tonight I could hold your gray eyes in mine
and tell you
what I've told myself here

The Longing

When he slipped on the mountain
I would have held him
but he chose the jolt of the rope

when the raft overturned in the canyon
he was confused   he went up
instead of down to my arms

I wait to the right   he turns left
I am on time   he is early or late
I whisper when he lies awake at night
he turns on a light   he pretends
he does not know me

I cannot forget his face
every day he becomes more beautiful
and my longing becomes harder to bear

but I wait
I know him better than he knows himself

I watch him walk in circles
lift his feet in the same worn tracks
all the time he comes to me
like a moth in love with the moon

I watch him read books
scratch words on paper
he will understand nothing
until he looks in my eyes

I watch him build his heap of things
find friends and lose them   couple and part
I am the one
always beyond his reach

I was with him in the darkness of the womb
they took him out screaming   he promised
to come back to me

when I step from behind that final tree
he will throw down everything   even his name
and before we lie down together
he will hold out the handful of blood
that remains from his birth   crying *here*

I carried it all the way for you

Return

What is this joy? That no animal
falters, but knows what it must do?
—Denise Levertov

When at one in the morning a raccoon
rustles out of the brush
and rises on hind legs peering
like a bear at my lamplit window,
swaying slightly, forelegs out-thrust,
then drops and walks its lumbering walk
into darkness, for a moment
I am wholer than before—
as if joined with the self
I am always losing, who is curious
and curiously sure, who embraces
all things in its calm regard,
never troubles itself
with forethought of death, and always
in the black light of darkness
sees its slow-stepping way.

Of Earth

for Wallace Stegner

Swallows looping and diving
by the darkening oaks, the flash
of their white bellies,
the tall grasses gathering last light,
glowing pale gold, silence
overflowing in a shimmer of breeze—
these could have happened
a different way. The heavy-trunked oaks
might not have branched and branched
and finely re-branched
as if to weave themselves into air.
There is no necessity
that any creature should fly,
that last light should turn
the grasses gold, that grasses
should exist at all,
or light.

　　　　　But a mind thinking so
is a mind wandering from home.
It is not thought that answers
each step of my feet, to be walking here
in the cool stir of dusk
is no mere possibility,
and I am so stained with the sweet
peculiar loveliness of things
that given God's power to dream worlds
from the dark, I know
I could only dream Earth—
birds, trees, this field of light
where I and each of us walk once.

FOUR

Naming The New One

They came from mountains and plains
to see the new one, the smooth-skin,
who stood on shaking hind legs
and stared, his eyes struck with light.

"He'll sleep cold," Bear grunted,
and walked away. Bigfoot
was already gone, scared,
and Hummingbird had things to do.

As the others walked and crawled
and flew by, the new one pointed
and hurled a sound at each of them,
louder and louder in his harsh joy.

"Those paws are no good," said Gopher.

"Call him *Wildmouth*," said Deer.
"Does he have ears?"

"He'll learn a song, maybe," said Owl.

Long after the new one stumbled away
they heard him crashing the brush,
still trailing his strange calls.

"Doesn't see where he's going,"
Cougar said.

"Well," said Coyote,
"we'll always know when he's *coming*."

He acted brave, but he was nervous.
"Let's watch him for a while.
There's plenty of room. When he finds
his place, then we'll name him."

The Apollo 17 Photo Of Earth

That shape called Africa,
that shape I learned from the Rand McNally World
on my bedroom wall, wondering
how do they know how continents look,

that image the word *Africa* makes
in millions of minds, that clear outline
of a thing never seen

is how it actually is—bulging West,
straight slant of Red Sea coast,
the graceful narrowing to Cape of Good Hope,
even Madagascar, the boot of Arabia—

only now I see no puzzle of pastels
but the tawny land itself, dappled, delicate as skin,
bright Sahara disappearing
around the western world-curve,

Africa shadowed in the south
with streamers and froth of thick white cloud
swirling up from Antarctica,

Africa floating not in pale map blue
but the blue of sea, deepest blue,
defining the land in one curved field,
                                    the planet

whole and shining in its black surround.

The Burden

The leather pack slides from my shoulders.
My friends and I have had long talks,
I know exactly what to do. I will start
the timer, run back the way I came,
and when the great light flares,
the brightest light ever seen,
the boiling red-black luminous cloud,
the world will renounce its wars.

But voices, laughter—suddenly
the woods are filled with roads and houses.
How, such an awful mistake. *We planned
carefully, I walked so far, alone—*

Vines and branches scratch, I crawl
clumsily over fallen trees, *farther*,
where no one lives. We planned,
I am sure we planned—*but I can't
remember, I can't remember
how it works*. Could an awkward step
set it off? A loud word? What sound
would the timer make? The woods are still.

Carefully I take off the pack
and hold it in my hands, a thing
I recognize, a thing I have never seen,
and as my fingers touch the buckles
I know: I carry Mystery, the secret
of stars and darkness, I carry
my death and the death of the world.
*But it isn't too late—
let it stay here, let it melt into ground.*

Quickly now,
back the way I came, to my friends,
a path appears, my feet move lightly,
lightly ahead—and there lies
the pack, exactly where I left it.
Running, running, the branches
woven against me, whipping my face,
I think I hear the timer ticking,
my feet sink into soft ground, I sprawl—
the pack is lying in front of me.

If I can take it apart and scatter
the pieces, harmless pieces—but
the pack is seamless, not leather
but the smoothest steel, nothing to grasp
but the timer switch. There's a shoebox
beside me, a worn paper sack,
a briefcase—boxes and bundles
are everywhere, I can't remember
which one it is, they are all
somehow mine, they spill from my arms...

I want to wake up now. I am carrying
what I can in a burlap bag. Shadows
are moving in the shadows of trees—
footsteps, the forest is filled with people.
We know each other, we call to each other,
we cannot speak without tears.
In bags, packs, wagons, baskets,
each of us is carrying the burden.
No one is leading, no one rests.
We are walking together
through the dim forest light.

Toward A New Science Fiction

None of us could explain
the pine that suddenly grew higher
and higher until its limbs
disappeared in blue
and we heard it stretching higher.

We cried out, watching for God
to come down, but nothing appeared
and slowly we calmed.
From all countries we gathered,
pressing hands and cheeks to the bark,
feeling infinity's faint shiver.

The climbers said there were new worlds
to settle, but in a few months
they all came back. The tree
kept going, they told us,
and it wasn't fear that stopped them,

but looking down day after day
as the curving sunlit swirl of Earth
shrank in the dark
until one hand could cover it—
if home wasn't there, they realized,
it wasn't anywhere.

Common Ground

Everywhere on Earth, wet beginnings:

fur, feather, scale, shell, skin, bone, blood,

like an infant discovering sound after sound
a voice is finding its tongue
in the slop and squall of birth.

                    It sounds,

and we, in whom Earth happened to light
a clear flame of consciousness,
are only beginning to learn the language—

who are made of the ash of stars,
who carry the sea we were born in,
who spent millions of years learning to breathe,
who shivered in fur at the reptiles' feet,
who trained our hands on the limbs of trees
and came down, slowly straightening
to look over the grasses, to see
that the world not only is
                    but is beautiful—

we are Earth learning to see itself,
to hear, touch, taste. What it wants to be
no one knows: finding a way
in starlight and dark, it begins in beauty,

                    it asks only time.

The Unborn of The Nuclear Age

Whatever they could be
is held in seed—
their faces
containing our faces
in the darkness deeper
than anyone can remember,
their voices
that given speech
will speak for us
when we have passed beyond speech—
whatever it is
the world wants to become
only they can tell,
only in them
can the womb speak its name
and only in us
can they speak at all,
they speak
if we speak for them.

The Windfall Oak

in memory of Ernie Arbuckle

Taking turns all morning with the screeching saw
we cut off the boughs
and work inward, lopping
the curved, green-lichened branches
into fireplace lengths.
Again and again the saw-bar sinks
through wood-flesh scribed with ring upon ring,
the careful memory of two hundred years.

In the storm's blast he listened in bed—
he heard the crack
of the half-hollowed trunk,
the long gesture of seed
completed by the wind's awful weight.

Now, his white hair specked with shavings,
he shuts off the saw.
We rest by the limb-stumps
in ringing quiet, the thick grass strewn
with heavy wealth—
not the only oak, not the biggest,
but one of the lives he joined
when he built his house here,
one of the lives that delighted his eyes
and the spirit eyes nourish,
the spirit refreshed by wholeness and grace.

In what deepened so slowly into earth and air,
we will slowly find
the best beauty we can: split wood tumbling

from the maul's clean stroke,
the fresh heaps weathering, fading
toward the color of ground,
and winters to come
the captive sun of all those seasons
leaping in the hearth,
the oak crumbling
to coals and ash, a blue spirit rising in the wind.

After The Wedding

for Marilyn

After the white balloons were swept away
on the wind that had swallowed
most of our vows, after the embraces
and tears, the flung rose petals,
after new friends and old friends and aunts
from everywhere, after you tossed
the bouquet, and the cries of the children
raised coyote cries on the rim,
after chicken grilled on juniper coals,
cold beer from the cattle trough
and hours of hot dancing to Beatles and Stones,
the last of us swaying arms on shoulders,
singing ourselves hoarse,
                 how good it is
to find you now beyond all
the loud joy, driving north in rain
and the lovely ease of our silence.

Dedication For A New Mirror

The raccoon I didn't see last night
I see this morning as you tell me,
I see her walk slowly across the porch
and scuttle back crouching, startled
at the one she suddenly sees
who crouches the same, who rears
and hisses exactly as she does,
a swaying stand-off. And now
she attacks, she jabs her sharp nose
almost to the mirror, and when the other
doesn't scare she scares herself—
scrunches her back, snarls, and at last
reaches forward, delicately pawing
the glass and peering behind it.

When it hangs on the bathroom door,
when we scan for mismatched colors
and new gray hairs, once in a while
let's remember her different way—
how she needed terribly to understand
who faced her, that one she knew, that stranger.

The Tidepool

In that clarity beneath our reflections
water-fleas darted, snails crept
among pink stones, a nickel-sized crab
slid sideways, crouched;
and running our hands through the forest
of blue-fringed weed, we found mussels
no bigger than a baby's thumbnail.
We'd been staring a long time
when we saw the barnacles fanning,
only inches deep—quick green plumes
shooting from the ordinary shells
and curling back, again and again,
each in its rhythm, thousands
of green feather-hands waving in
what the water provided.
But it was more than feeding,
it was a kind of speech, a chant of green
as strange and suddenly clear
as ourselves, belly-down on the worn granite
of this speck carried somewhere
in the drift of stars. Nothing
out there in that pool of dark,
none of those points of icy fire
can tell us where we are,
or why. If we had eyes that could see
a trillion light-years, the galaxies
would blur to a hazy glow—
and we'd know less than whatever was told
in those green exclamations
the barnacles made, strange and clear,
only inches away, almost overlooked.
As we lay there watching,
to be alive as we are wasn't all I wanted
but enough: lost in this plenty,
small enough to see.

Ourselves

When the throaty calls of sandhill cranes
echo across the valley, when the rimrock flares
incandescent red, and the junipers
are flames of green on the shortgrass hills,

in that moment of last clear light
when the world seems ready to speak its name,
meet me in the field alongside the pond.
Without careers for once, without things to do,

without dreams or anger or the rattle of fears,
we'll ask how it can be that we walk this ground
and know that we walk, alive in a world
that didn't have to be beautiful, alive

in a world that doesn't have to be.
With no answers, just ourselves and silence,
we'll listen for the song that waits to be learned,
the song that moves through the passing light.

Biographical Note

John Daniel grew up near Washington, D.C. and moved to the Northwest in the late 1960's. He attended Reed College worked as a logger, railroader, and rock-climbing instructor, and lived on a ranch in eastern Oregon for several years. In 1982 he received a Wallace Stegner Fellowship in Poetry at Stanford University, where he then taught creative writing for five years as a Jones Lecturer. As well as poems, Daniel writes essays and articles on conservation and the environment. He and his wife Marilyn, an environmental engineer, live near Portland, Oregon.